TATTED SNOWFLAKES

Vida Sunderman

DOVER PUBLICATIONS, INC.
Garden City, New York

*To my daughter Gloria for her encouragement and help
in designing the snowflakes and writing this book.*

Artwork for Figures 1–14 by Gregory Guiteras.

Copyright

Designs and text copyright © 1995 by Vida Sunderman.
Line drawings for Figures 1–14 copyright © 1995 by Dover Publications, Inc.
All rights reserved.

Bibliographical Note

Tatted Snowflakes is a new work, first published by Dover Publications, Inc. in 1995.

Library of Congress Cataloging-in-Publication Data

Sunderman, Vida.
    Tatted snowflakes / Vida Sunderman.
        p. cm.—(Dover needlework series)
    ISBN-13: 978-0-486-28303-6
    ISBN-10: 0-486-28303-8
    1. Tatting—Patterns. 2. Snowflakes in art. I. Title. II. Series.

TT840.T38S86 1995
745.594'12—dc20

                                                                    94-39845
                                                                    CIP

Manufactured in the United States by LSC Communications
28303817   2020
www.doverpublications.com

Introduction

Today there is a renewal of interest in tatting—the art of making lace with a shuttle, thread and your fingers. The lace is fragile and delicate in appearance, but very strong. The fragile appearance is very appropriate for snowflakes, giving them a lacy, snowy look.

Shuttles

There are several kinds of shuttles available today in craft and variety stores. Here are a few of my favorites.

Susan Bates has a small plastic shuttle with a sharp point that works well with tatting thread or other fine thread. The red Boye shuttle is a medium-sized shuttle with a point and is my favorite for size 10 or 20 thread. Tatsy makes a large shuttle suitable for heavier threads or fine yarn. It does not have a point on it, so a crochet hook is needed for joining rings or chains to picots.

All of these shuttles are made with a shank that has a hole in it to fasten the thread. The thread is wound around the shank.

There are also metal shuttles available with removable bobbins. The thread is wound on the bobbin, which is then inserted into the shuttle. Extra bobbins may be purchased, so the thread can be changed by changing the bobbin. These shuttles generally have a hook on the end.

Other types of shuttles are available in a wide range of materials from plastic to silver.

Thread

Thread that is smooth and strong works best for tatting. Most crochet threads, available in craft and variety stores, are suitable for tatting. The size of the thread used determines the size of the finished snowflake. Size 10 or bedspread-weight thread makes a large-size snowflake. Medium-size snowflakes can be made with size 20 or 30 crochet thread. Miniature snowflakes, dainty and fragile in appearance, are made with tatting thread (size 70 or 80). Specialty threads can be used to give a distinctive look to your work. Ribbon floss, for example, gives a soft, satiny finish.

Learn How to Tat

Rings, chains and picots are the basic components of tatting. There is just one basic stitch—the double stitch. The double stitch is made in two parts around a base thread.

To start tatting you will need a shuttle, two contrasting colors of size 10 or bedspread-weight thread, small scissors and a small crochet hook if your shuttle does not have a hook or point on it. A sewing needle to pick out the stitches when a mistake is made is helpful, along with a lot of patience, practice and persistence.

Start learning to tat by making a chain. A chain requires a shuttle thread and a base or ball thread. We will use white and blue thread for our example. Wind the white thread onto the shuttle. The blue thread will be the base or ball thread. Tie the ends of the white and blue threads together with a square knot (page 6). Hold the knot between the thumb and index finger of your left hand. Place the blue thread over the fingers of the left hand and wrap it around your little finger four or five times. Hold the shuttle between the thumb and index finger of your right hand in a horizontal position, with the point toward your left hand and the thread coming from the back of the shuttle (Fig. 1).

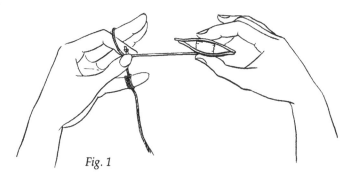

Fig. 1

To make the first half of the double stitch, put the thread from the shuttle over the fingers of your right hand, then slide the shuttle under the base thread between the index finger and the middle finger of your left hand (Fig. 2).

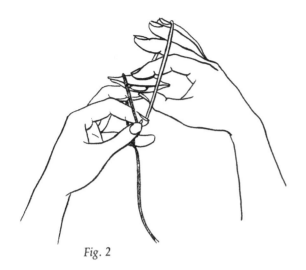

Fig. 2

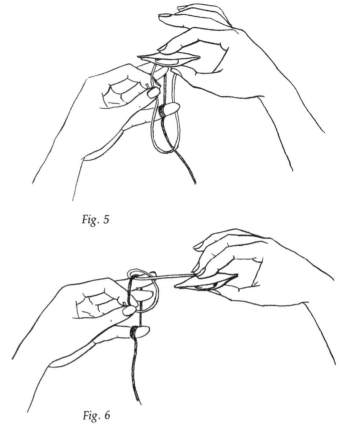

Fig. 5

Bring the shuttle back over the base thread and through the loop formed by the shuttle thread that was over the right hand (*Fig. 3*).

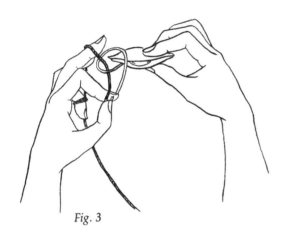

Fig. 3

Now it is necessary to transfer the loop to the base (blue) thread that is over the fingers of your left hand. To do this, drop the middle finger of the left hand slightly and pull the shuttle thread taut with the right hand. The thread will snap, forming a loop in the base thread. Raise the middle fingers of the left hand to slide the loop up to the knot between the thumb and index finger. This is the first half of the double stitch (*Fig. 4*).

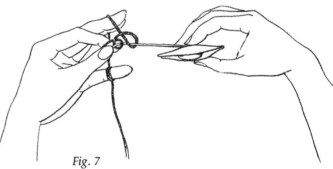

Fig. 6

To make the second half of the double stitch, slide the shuttle over the top of the base thread between the index and middle fingers of the left hand (*Fig. 5*), then slide it back under the thread and through the loop of shuttle (white) thread below the fingers (*Fig. 6*).

Transfer the loop to the base thread as before. Slide the loop next to the first half of the stitch. This completes one double stitch (*Fig. 7*).

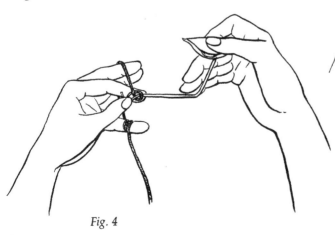

Fig. 7

To make a ring, only the shuttle thread is needed. Wind the shuttle, leaving 18" of thread free. Grasp the thread 3" from the end with the thumb and index finger of your left hand. Wrap the thread over and around the fingers of the left hand, holding it between the thumb and index finger. The thread will make a complete circle around your fingers (*Fig. 8*).

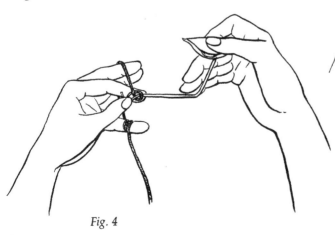

Fig. 4

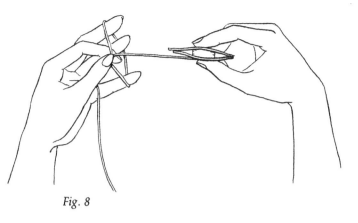

Fig. 8

Make the double stitch as for the chain. If the stitch is made correctly, it will move on the base thread. Keep making double stitches around the base thread as specified in the pattern. As you need more thread around your fingers, unwind it from the shuttle and pull on the thread between your thumb and little finger. If there is too much thread around the fingers, pull on the shuttle thread to make the ring smaller. When the specified number of stitches has been made, pull on the shuttle thread to form the stitches into a ring.

Picots

A picot is a loop of thread between two double stitches. Picots are used as a decoration, or to join rings and chains to each other, helping to form a design. The length of a picot depends on the size of the thread used. Heavier thread takes a longer picot, while a smaller picot is made with finer thread. The length of a picot used for decoration is a matter of choice.

The picot is formed by leaving a space between the double stitches. To practice it, make 2 double stitches on a ring, then make the first half of the next double stitch, stopping ¼" from the previous double stitch. Make the second half of the double stitch (*Fig. 9*). Slide this double stitch next to the previous one, forming a loop called the picot (*Fig. 10*).

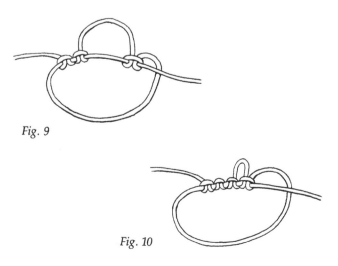

Fig. 9

Fig. 10

The picot spacing given in a pattern is the amount of space that is to be left between double stitches. Using a guide, it is easy to make long picots all the same length. For 1" spacing, use a small ruler or stick as a guide. Place the ruler between the base thread (thread over your fingers) and the shuttle thread, next to the last stitch made, then make the next double stitch. Remove the ruler and push the double stitches together, forming the picot.

Wooden ice cream sticks make a good ½" guide, or you can cut a strip about 2" long and the desired width from a plastic lid.

Reverse Work

To reverse your work, turn it upside down so that the base of the ring or chain is at the top. You usually reverse the work between rings and chains so that the stitches are facing the proper direction (*Figs. 11 and 12*).

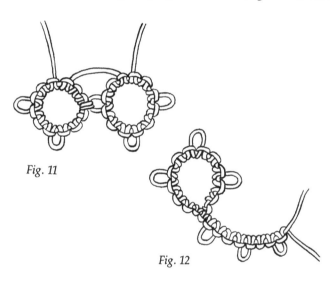

Fig. 11

Fig. 12

Joining

To join one ring or chain to another, draw a loop of thread through the joining picot large enough for the shuttle to slide through. Slide the shuttle through the loop (*Fig. 13*). Pull the shuttle thread next to the picot so that it resembles the first half of the double stitch. This joining stitch counts as the first half of the next stitch. Make the second half of the double stitch. This stitch counts as the first stitch of the next group of stitches.

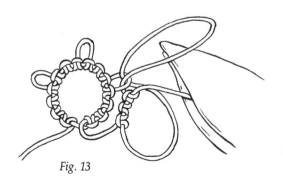

Fig. 13

5

Fold-Over Join

A fold-over join is used to join the last ring or chain of a motif to the first ring or chain of the motif. Fold the first ring over from right to left above the joining picot. Insert the hook or point of the shuttle *under* the joining picot of the first ring or chain, make a twist in the picot and draw the base thread (the thread over your fingers) through the picot, making a loop large enough for the shuttle to go through. Insert the shuttle through the loop and draw the thread up to the joining picot to form the first half of the double stitch. Complete the ring or chain.

The Square Knot

A square knot is used to tie the shuttle and ball threads together, to tie the threads together at the end of a project and to join a new thread when the shuttle is empty and more thread is needed.

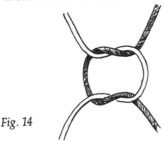

Fig. 14

To practice making a square knot, use a white thread and a dark-colored one. With the dark thread in your right hand and the white in your left hand, cross the white thread over the dark thread. Wrap the end of white thread around the dark thread. Cross the ends of the threads again, having the white thread over the dark thread. Wrap the end of white thread through the loop formed and around the dark thread. Pull ends together tightly. If a square knot is tied correctly it will not come undone. *Fig. 14* shows the square knot before the ends are pulled together.

If you need to join a new thread in the middle of your work, it is best to tie it on after a ring or chain is made. Clip the ends of the threads about 1½" long and work them into the next ring or chain as it is being made by drawing the end through the loop in the base thread. Do this for 3 or 4 stitches. A new thread cannot be tied on in the middle of a ring since the knot will not pull through the stitches when the ring is closed.

Using Two Shuttles

Sometimes, in order to make the stitches lie flat, it is necessary to use two shuttles. Either shuttle can hold the base thread. The shuttle designated for use in the instructions is the *active* shuttle, or the one used in the right hand. The other shuttle is used as the base or ball thread.

To identify which shuttle is to be used as #1 or #2, use shuttles of different colors or mark them with small pieces of masking tape.

The Continuous Thread

Mlle. Riego, an English needlework artist, wrote eleven tatting books between 1850 and 1868. She developed many techniques that are still used today. One of her most important developments was the use of a continuous thread. After winding the shuttle, she did not cut the thread from the ball. Instead, she started to tat in the middle of the thread between the shuttle and ball. Using the continuous thread method eliminates the need to finish two ends of thread. The fewer ends you have, the neater your work.

The patterns in this book use the continuous thread method by stating the amount of thread needed for the shuttle. Measure the amount of thread needed for the shuttle and tie a loop loosely at this point. Wind the thread on the shuttle, leaving 18" free to wrap around your fingers. Do not cut the thread if the ball thread is to be used. Untie the loop and start tatting at this point.

If two shuttles are used, measure the correct amount of thread for the first shuttle and tie a loop loosely at this point. Wind it on the shuttle, leave 18" free. Starting at the loop, measure the yardage needed for the second shuttle and cut it from the ball. Starting with the cut end, wind this thread on the second shuttle, stopping 18" from the loop. Untie the loop and start tatting at this point. If two colors of thread are used, you cannot use the continuous method, because the threads will have to be tied together to start tatting.

The amount of thread needed on a shuttle will vary if a different size thread is used. A finer thread takes less, a heavier thread takes more. The size of the picots can also vary the amount of thread needed.

Correcting Mistakes

Tatting does not unravel; each stitch is a knot. If a mistake is made, and just a few stitches need to be undone, the stitches may be picked out with a sewing needle or the point of the shuttle. The shuttle must be reversed through the enlarged stitch.

If there is a only a small amount of thread on the shuttle, unwind it, and pull the base thread backward through the stitches until the mistake is undone.

It is difficult to open a ring, but it *is* possible. Hold the ring in the same position as when you made it. Separate the stitches at a picot and pull on the base thread between the stitches until you have a small loop. Then pull on the base thread where the first and last stitches of the ring meet until the loop is large enough for the shuttle to pass through. The stitches will then need to be undone one by one.

If a mistake is made earlier in the snowflake, cut the stitches after the mistake leaving 2 or 3 rings and chains. Do *not* cut picots. Pull the base thread from the rings and chains until you have undone the mistake. Tie on a new thread and continue making the snowflake.

Finishing Ends

When a snowflake is completed, cut the thread leaving 4" ends; tie them in a square knot. With a small sewing needle and matching thread, whipstitch the ends to the back of the snowflake for ⅜", working each end in a different direction. Cut the ends close to the snowflake.

Another method of finishing is to glue the ends to the back of the snowflake. Cut the ends to ⅜". Squeeze a small amount of glue on a piece of paper and, using a toothpick, spread the glue on the snowflake in the appropriate place. Hold the ends in place until they are secure.

If a heavier thread is used, cut the thread leaving 4" ends; tie in a square knot. Unwind the end of thread and use one strand threaded on a small sewing needle to whipstitch the rest of the thread to the back of the snowflake for ⅜". Work the thread on the needle under 2 stitches. Repeat with the other end of the thread. Cut the ends close to the snowflake.

Laundering Snowflakes

To launder snowflakes, use a small jar or plastic container with a tight-fitting lid. Add softened lukewarm water and a mild detergent or soap such as liquid Woolite or Ivory Flakes. Add a gentle bleach if the snowflake is stained or discolored. A natural bleach is lemon juice and water. Hydrogen peroxide will remove some stains. Shake the jar well to dissolve the soap. Add the snowflake and shake well. If the snowflake is stained, leave it in the solution until the stain disappears, but be sure to check it often. Do not bleach any longer than necessary. Rinse by filling the jar with cold water and shaking the snowflake in it. Repeat two or more times. Place the snowflake between layers of a Turkish towel or between white paper towels to remove excess water; do not wring or twist. Place the snowflake on a padded surface or towel; shape and straighten picots while the snowflake is still damp or starch and block if desired.

Blocking Snowflakes

Blocking gives your tatting a professional finish.

Copy the appropriate blocking diagram on page 8 onto white paper. If the snowflake measures more than 3" across, extend the lines as long as necessary.

Laundry starch, corn starch, sugar starch or fabric stiffener purchased at variety or craft stores may be used to starch the snowflakes. White glue diluted with an equal amount of water is also suitable. Saturate the snowflake with the starch solution. Remove excess starch by placing the snowflake between layers of white paper toweling and patting it. Do not wring or twist.

Place the blocking diagram on a padded surface and cover it with plastic wrap. With rustproof pins, pin the snowflake over the diagram. Straighten the picots. Let the snowflake dry completely before removing it. Laundry or cornstarch may be dried by ironing. Sugar starch must be air dried, but a blow dryer may be used to hasten the process. If you have used a fabric stiffener, follow the directions on the bottle.

Working With Beads

To string small seed beads (known as *rocaille* beads) onto size 10 thread, dip the end of the ball thread in white glue for 2". Let it dry completely. Before starting to tat, use the glued end of the thread as a needle and string the beads on the ball thread. If the end becomes frayed, just snip it off. Wind the amount of thread needed onto the shuttle, moving the beads along the thread. Do not cut the thread between the shuttle and ball thread.

To make a chain with beads, the beads are used from the ball thread. A few beads are held on the thread on the back of the fingers of the left hand between the index and little fingers. Following pattern directions, a bead is pushed up to the last double stitch made and is held in place by the next double stitch. More beads are moved up to the back of the fingers as needed.

To use beads in a ring, string them onto the shuttle thread. A large shuttle works best. Estimate the amount of thread needed between beads and wind this on the shuttle. Then move a bead or the number of beads needed in a group onto the shuttle. Repeat the process until all beads are used. Keep the beads on the shuttle until one or a group is needed.

Decorating with Snowflakes

Use your imagination and dream up the many places you can use snowflakes. Here are a few suggestions.

- Snowflakes give a lacy, frosty look to a Christmas tree.
- Miniature snowflakes can be used to decorate a small artificial tree.
- Have a gift tree of snowflakes and let each guest pick one from the tree. It saves time, work and the cost of wrapping gifts.
- Tie snowflakes evenly spaced on a red ribbon to make a garland. Fasten the garland to the mantel of a fireplace or hang it in a window.
- Scatter several small suction cups with hooks on a window. Hang snowflakes on the hooks.
- Decorate Christmas packages with snowflakes. Glue them on in only a couple of places so they can be removed and used as a decoration by the recipient.
- Glue a miniature snowflake on a sheet of stationery to make a unique Christmas letter.
- Enclose a snowflake in a Christmas card for special friends.
- Use a floral pick to hold a snowflake and tuck it in a poinsettia plant or flower arrangement.
- Tack small snowflakes around the base of a candle with small craft pins to make a centerpiece.
- Lay a wide red ribbon down the center of your table and place snowflakes on top for a festive touch.

Abbreviations

b(s)	beads(s)
beg	beginning
ch	chain
cl r	close ring
corresp	corresponding
ds	double stitch
lg ch	long chain
lg p	long picot
lp	loop
lrg r	large ring
prev	previous
r	ring
rem	remaining
rep	repeat
rnd	round
rw	reverse work
sep	separated
sh	shuttle
sk	skip
sm p	small picot
sm r	small ring
sp	space
tog	together
yd(s).	yard(s)

The instructions between ( ) are to be repeated the number of times stated.

The instructions following an * are to be repeated the number of times stated, plus the original amount stated.

BLOCKING DIAGRAMS

Six-sided Snowflake

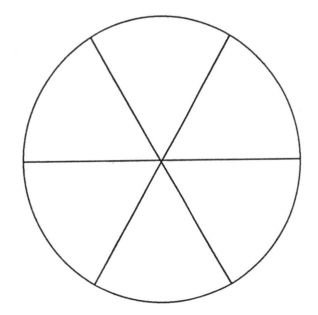

Star-shaped Snowflake

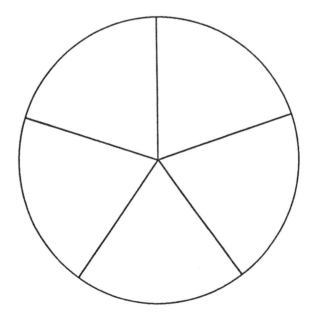

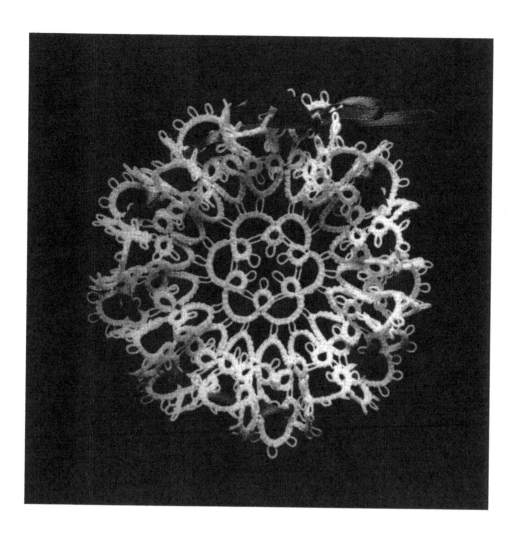

Ruffled Snowflake

Approximately 3¾" in diameter

Materials:
Size 20 white thread.
Shuttle.
½ yd. ⅛"-wide red satin ribbon.

Rnd 1: Wind 1½ yds. on shuttle, do not cut; use ball thread.
R of 3 ds, (p, 3 ds) 3 times, cl r; rw. Ch 3 ds, (p, 3 ds) 3 times; rw. *R of 3 ds, join to last p of prev r, 3 ds, (p, 3 ds) twice, cl r; rw. Ch 3 ds, (p, 3 ds) 3 times; rw. Rep from * around up to the last p of 6th r, join to first p of first r, 3 ds, cl r; rw. Make ch and join at base of first r. Cut and tie.

Rnd 2: Wind 6½ yds. on shuttle, do not cut; use ball thread.
*R of 3 ds, (p, 3 ds) 3 times, cl r. Rep from * once more; rw. Ch 6 ds, join to any p on Rnd 1, 6 ds; rw. **R of 3 ds, p, 3 ds, join to middle p of prev r, 3 ds, p, 3 ds, cl r. R of 3 ds, (p, 3 ds) 3 times. Ch 6 ds, join to next p on Rnd 1, 6 ds; rw. Rep from ** until you have made 35 rings. Make 36th r of 3 ds, p, 3 ds, fold-over join to middle p of first r, 3 ds, p, 3 ds, cl r; rw. Ch 6 ds, join to last p on Rnd 1, 6 ds, join at base of first r. Cut and tie.

Rnd 3: Wind 7 yds. on shuttle, do not cut; use ball thread.
R of 3 ds, p, 3 ds, join to any free p on Rnd 2, 3 ds, p, 3 ds, cl r; rw. Ch 3 ds, (p, 3 ds) 3 times; rw. *R of 3 ds, p, 3 ds, join to next free p on Rnd 2, 3 ds, p, 3 ds, cl r; rw. Ch 3 ds, (p, 3 ds) 3 times; rw. Rep from * around, join at base of first r. Cut and tie.

Starch and block, having 2 rings on Rnd 3 flat on the blocking surface and the next 2 rings raised; continue around. When the snowflake is dry, weave red ribbon through the rings in Rnd 3. Start weaving by inserting the ribbon from front to back through 1 flat ring, (sk 2 raised rings, insert ribbon back to front through next flat ring and front to back through next flat ring); rep around, tie ribbon in a bow.

Elegant Snowflake

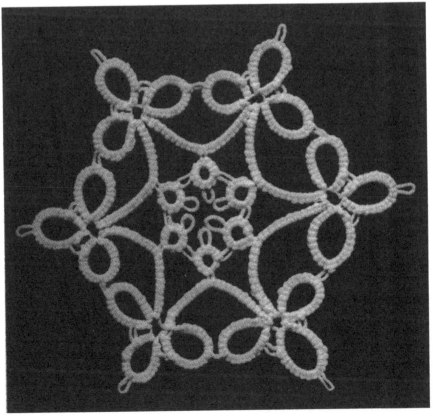

Trefoil Snowflake

Elegant Snowflake

Approximately 4½" point to point

Materials:
Size 20 white thread.
2 shuttles.

Wind 7 yds. on Sh #1, do not cut; wind 6 yds. on Sh #2.
Sh #1, r of 3 ds, (p, 3 ds) 3 times, cl r; rw. Ch 4 ds, p, 4 ds; rw. R of 2 ds, join to last p of prev r, (2 ds, p) twice, 2 ds, cl r; rw. Ch 4 ds, p, 4 ds. *Sh #2*, r of 3 ds, (p, 3 ds) 3 times, cl r. *Sh #1*, ch 4 ds, p, 4 ds; rw. R of 2 ds, p, 2 ds, join to middle p of corresp r on opposite side, 2 ds, p, 2 ds, cl r; rw. Ch 4 ds, p, 4 ds; rw. R of 3 ds, join to last p of prev r, 3 ds, join to middle p of next r on opposite side, 3 ds, p, 3 ds, cl r; rw. Ch 4 ds, p, 4 ds; rw.** R of 3 ds, sm p, 3 ds, cl r; rw. Ch 4 ds, sm p, 4 ds; rw. Sm r of 3 ds, lg p, 3 ds, cl r; rw. Ch 4 ds, join to sm p of prev ch, 4 ds; rw. R of 3 ds, sm p, 3 ds, cl r; rw. Ch 4 ds, join to p of corresp ch, 4 ds; rw. ***Rep from * to ** once. R of 3 ds, join to sm p of corresp r on opposite side, 3 ds, cl r; rw. Ch 4 ds, sm p, 4 ds; rw. R of 3 ds, join to lg p of first r in center of snowflake, 3 ds, cl r; rw. Ch 4 ds, join to sm p of prev ch, 4 ds; rw. R of 3 ds, sm p, 3 ds, cl r; rw. Ch 4 ds, join to p of corresp ch, 4 ds; rw. Rep from *** 4 more times, joining last r of last rep to sm p of corresp r on opposite side. Work last ch and join at base of first r. Cut and tie.

Trefoil Snowflake

Approximately 4¼" point to point

Materials:
Size 10 white thread.
2 shuttles.

Wind 9 yds. on Sh #1, do not cut; wind 4 yds. on Sh #2.
Sh #1, r of 12 ds, p, 9 ds, p, 3 ds, cl r. *R of 3 ds, join to last p of prev r, (9 ds, p) twice, 3 ds, cl r. R of 3 ds, join to last p of prev r, 9 ds, p, 12 ds, cl r; rw. Ch 11 ds.* *Sh #2*, sm r of 3 ds, (p, 3 ds) 3 times, cl r. ***Sh #1*, ch 11 ds, rw. R of 12 ds, join to free p of last Sh #1 ring, 9 ds, p, 3 ds, cl r. Rep from * to * once. *Sh #2*, sm r of 3 ds, join to last p of prev sm r, (3 ds, p) twice, 3 ds, cl r. Rep from ** 3 more times. For 4th rep: *Sh #1*, ch 11 ds, rw. R of 12 ds, join to free p of last Sh #1 r, 9 ds, p, 3 ds, cl r. R of 3 ds, join to last p of prev r, (9 ds, p) twice, 3 ds, cl r. R of 3 ds, join to last p of prev r, 9 ds, fold-over join to first p of first r, 12 ds, cl r; rw. Ch 11 ds. *Sh #2*, sm r of 3 ds, join to last p of prev sm r, 3 ds, p, 3 ds, join to first p of first sm r, 3 ds, cl r. *Sh #1*, ch 11 ds, join at base of first r. Cut and tie.

Ruffle-Edged Snowflake

Ruffle-Edged Snowflake

Approximately 3" point to point

Materials:
Size 20 white thread.
2 shuttles.

Rnd 1: Wind 1½ yds. on shuttle, do not cut; use ball thread.
R of 2 ds, 3 p sep by 4 ds, 2 ds, cl r; rw. *Ch 2 ds, rw. R of 2 ds, join to last p of prev r, (4 ds, p) twice, 2 ds, cl r; rw. Rep from * until you have made 5 rings and chains. R of 2 ds, join to last p of prev r, 4 ds, p, 4 ds, fold-over join to first p of first r, 2 ds, cl r; rw. Ch 2 ds, join at base of first r. Cut and tie.

Rnd 2: Wind 1 yd. on Sh #1, do not cut; wind 4½ yds. on Sh #2.
Sh #1, join thread in p between rings, ch 4 ds, 3 p sep by 2 ds, 4 ds. *Sh #2*, r of 2 ds, (p, 2 ds) 5 times, cl r. *Sh #1*, ch 4 ds, 3 p sep by 2 ds, 4 ds, join in p between next 2 rings. Ch 4 ds, 3 p sep by 2 ds, 4 ds. Rep from * around, join in same p as first joining.

Rnd 3: Note—One *group* = ch first half of ds 4 times, then last half of ds 4 times. A joining st does not count as part of a group.
Wind 1 yd. on shuttle, do not cut; use ball thread.
Join in middle p of any ch before a r on Rnd 2. *Ch 2 groups, join in 2nd p of next r. Ch 2 groups, p, 2 groups, sk 1 p on r, join in next p. Ch 2 groups, join in 2nd p of next ch. Ch 1 group, join in 2nd p of next ch. Rep from * around. Cut and tie.

Minaret Snowflake

Approximately 3¾" point to point

Materials:
Size 10 white thread.
2 shuttles.

Rnd 1: Wind 2 yds. on shuttle, do not cut; use ball thread.
*R of 3 ds, (p, 3 ds) 3 times, cl r; rw. Ch 3 ds, p, 1 ds, lg p, 1 ds, p, 3 ds; rw. Rep from * 5 more times. Join at base of first r. Cut and tie.

Rnd 2: Wind 2 yds. on Sh #1, do not cut; wind 4 yds. on Sh #2.
Sh #1, r of 3 ds, p, 3 ds, join to middle p of any r on Rnd 1, 3 ds, p, 3 ds, cl r; rw. **Sh #2*, r of 2 ds, p, 1 ds, lg p, 1 ds, p, 2 ds, cl r. *Sh #1*, ch 3 ds, (p, 3 ds) 3 times, join to next free p on same r on Rnd 1, ch 3 ds, join to first p of next r, ch 3 ds, (p, 3 ds) 3 times;** rw. R of 3 ds, p, 3 ds, join to middle p of same r on Rnd 1, 3 ds, p, 3 ds, cl r; rw. Rep from * 4 more times. For 5th rep work from * to **, join at base of first r. Cut and tie.

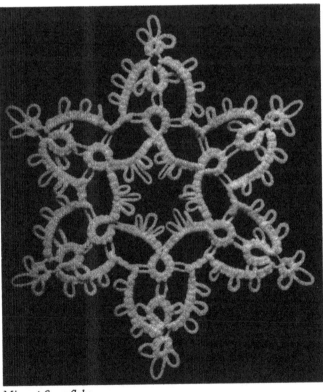

Minaret Snowflake

Ribbon-Floss Snowflake

Approximately 2¾" point to point

Materials:
White ribbon floss.
2 shuttles.

Rnd 1: Wind 1 yd. on shuttle. Lg p spacing is ½".
R of 1 ds, (lg p, 1 ds) 12 times, cl r. Cut and tie.

Ribbon-Floss Snowflake

Rnd 2: Wind 1½ yds. on Sh #1, do not cut; wind 3½ yds. on Sh #2.
Sh #1, r of 3 ds, join to any p on Rnd 1, 3 ds, cl r; rw. *Ch 2 ds, (p, 2 ds) twice. *Sh #2*, r of 3 ds, (p, 3 ds) 3 times, cl r. *Sh #1*, ch 2 ds, (p, 2 ds) twice,** rw. R of 3 ds, sk 1 p on Rnd 1, join to next p, 3 ds, cl r; rw. Rep from * around, end last rep at **. Join at base of first r. Cut and tie.
Note: Do not starch snowflake as it takes away the sheen of the ribbon.

Tiny Snowflake

Approximately 1½" point to point

Materials:
Size 30 white thread.
Shuttle.

Rnd 1: Wind ½ yd. on shuttle, do not cut; use ball thread.
R of 1 ds, (sm p, 1 ds) 6 times, cl r. Cut and tie.
Rnd 2: Wind 1 yd. on shuttle, do not cut; use ball thread.
R of 2 ds, p, 2 ds, join to any p on Rnd 1, 2 ds, p, 2 ds, cl r; rw. *Ch 2 ds, (p, 2 ds) twice, lg p, (2 ds, p) twice, 2 ds; rw. R of 2 ds, join to last p of prev r, 2 ds, join to next p on Rnd 1, 2 ds, p, 2 ds; cl r. Rep from * 3 more times. Ch 2 ds, (p, 2 ds) twice, lg p, (2 ds, p) twice, 2 ds; rw. R of 2 ds, join to last p of prev r, 2 ds, join to next p on Rnd 1, 2 ds, join to first p of first r, 2 ds, cl r; rw. Make ch as before. Join at base of first r. Cut and tie.

12

Ruffled-Star Snowflake

Approximately 3¾" point to point

Materials:
Size 10 white thread.
2 shuttles.

Center Ring: Wind 1 yd. on shuttle.
R of 1 ds, 6 p sep by 2 ds, 1 ds, cl r. Cut and tie.
Rnd 1: *Note*—1 *group* = ch first half of ds 4 times, then 2nd half of ds 4 times.
Wind 3 yds. on Sh #1, do not cut; wind 5½ yds. on Sh #2.
Sh #1, r of 2 ds, p, 2 ds, join to any p on Center Ring, 2 ds, p, 2 ds, cl r; rw. *Ch 2 groups. Sh #2*, r of 2 ds, (p, 2 ds) 3 times, cl r. R of 2 ds, join to last p of prev r, (2 ds, p) 4 times, 2 ds, cl r. R of 2 ds, join to last p of prev r, (2 ds, p) twice, 2 ds, cl r. *Sh #1*, ch 2 groups, rw.** R of 2 ds, p, 2 ds, join to next p on Center Ring, 2 ds, p, 2 ds, cl r; rw. Rep from * around, end last rep at **, join at base of first r. Cut and tie.

Ruffled-Star Snowflake

Flower Snowflake

Approximately 4" point to point

Materials:
Size 20 white thread.
Shuttle.

Center Ring: Wind 1 yd. on shuttle. P has ½" spacing.
R of 1 ds, (p, 1 ds) 12 times, cl r. Cut and tie.
Petal Rnd: Wind 10 yds. on shuttle, do not cut; use ball thread.
R of 3 ds, join to any p on Center Ring, 3 ds, cl r; rw. Ch 3 ds, rw. R of 3 ds, sm p, 3 ds, cl r. R of 5 ds, p, 5 ds, cl r; rw. Ch 2 ds, (p, 2 ds) 3 times; rw. **R of 5 ds, join to p of prev r, 5 ds, cl r. R of 7 ds, p, 7 ds, cl r; rw. Ch 2 ds, (p, 2 ds) 5 times; rw. R of 7 ds, join to p of prev r, 7 ds, cl r; rw. *Ch 2 ds, (p, 2 ds) 5 times; rw. R of 7 ds, join to same p as before, 7 ds, cl r; rw. Rep from * once more, but *do not rw.* R of 5 ds, join to next joining p, 5 ds, cl r; rw.† Ch 2 ds, (p, 2 ds) 3 times; rw. R of 5 ds, join to same p as before, 5 ds, cl r. R of 3 ds, join to sm p of r on opposite side, 3 ds, cl r; rw. Ch 3 ds, rw. R of 3 ds, sk 1 p on Center Ring, join to next p, 3 ds, cl r; rw. Ch 3 ds, rw. R of 3 ds, sm p, 3 ds, cl r. R of 5 ds, p, 5 ds, cl r; rw. Ch 2 ds, join to first p of next ch on opposite side, (2 ds, p) twice, 2 ds; rw. Rep from ** 4 more times. Rep from ** to † once more, ch 2 ds, (p, 2 ds) twice, fold-over join to first p of corresp ch on beg repeat, 2 ds; rw. R of 5 ds, join to same p as before, 5 ds, cl r. R of 3 ds, join to sm p of r on opposite side, 3 ds, cl r; rw. Ch 3 ds, join at base of first r. Cut and tie.

Flower Snowflake

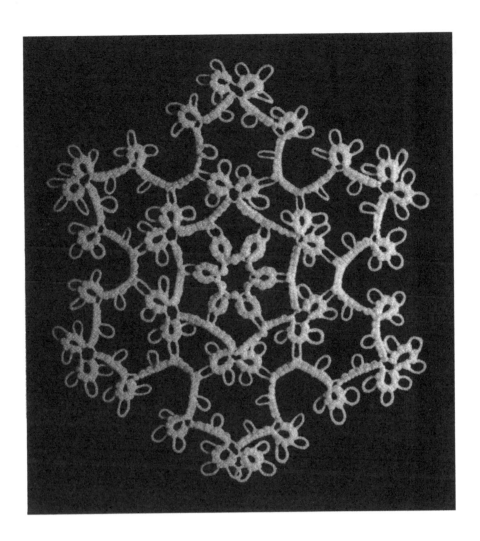

Little Ring Snowflake

Approximately 4½" point to point

Materials:
Size 10 white thread.
Shuttle.

Rnd 1: Wind 1½ yds. on shuttle, do not cut; use ball thread.
*R of 4 ds, p, 4 ds, cl r; rw. Ch 2 ds, rw. Rep from * 5 more times, join at base of first r. Cut and tie.

Rnd 2: Wind 2½ yds. on shuttle, do not cut; use ball thread.
*R of 2 ds, (p, 2 ds) 3 times, cl r. Rep from * once more; rw. Ch 5 ds, join to p of any r on first rnd, 5 ds; rw. Rep from * around, joining chs to p of each succeeding r of first rnd. Join last ch at base of first r. Cut and tie.

Rnd 3: Wind 4½ yds. on shuttle, do not cut; use ball thread.
**R of 2 ds, (p, 2 ds) 3 times, cl r; rw. Ch 3 ds, p, 3 ds; rw.
*R of 2 ds, (p, 2 ds) 3 times, cl r. Rep from * once more; rw. Ch 3 ds, p, 3 ds; rw. R of 2 ds, (p, 2 ds) 3 times, cl r; rw. Ch 3 ds, p, 3 ds, join to middle p of first r on Rnd 2

(*see diagram*), ch 4 ds, join to middle p of next r on Rnd 2. Ch 3 ds, p, 3 ds; rw. Rep from ** 5 more times, joining 3rd ch of each rep to middle p of next r on Rnd 2. Join last ch at base of first r. Cut and tie.

Join Rnd 3 here ——

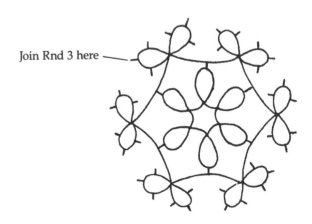

14

Bejewelled Snowflake

Approximately 3½" point to point

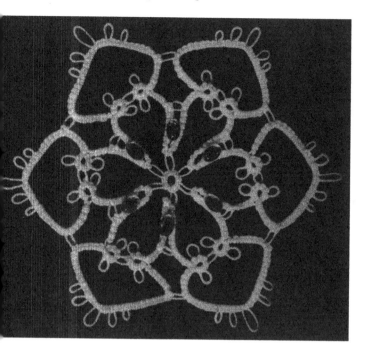

Materials:
Size 20 white thread.
Shuttle.
Six 6mm × 4 mm crystal oval acrylic stones.
Glue.

Wind 3 yds. on shuttle, do not cut; use ball thread.

Center Ring: R of 2 ds, (p, 2 ds) 5 times, cl r; tie ball and sh threads together to form 6th p. Count knot as first half of next ds.

Rnd 1: Ch 8 ds, p, 4 ds; rw. R of 2 ds, (p, 2 ds) 3 times, cl r; rw. Lg ch of 6 ds, p, *8 ds, sm p, 3 ds, medium p, 3 ds, lg p, 3 ds, medium p, 3 ds, sm p, 8 ds, p, 6 ds; rw. R of 2 ds, p, 2 ds, join to middle p of prev r, 2 ds, p, 2 ds, cl r; rw. Ch 4 ds, p, 8 ds, join in next p on Center Ring, inserting shuttle from front to back through joining loop. Ch 8 ds, join in p of prev ch, 4 ds; rw. R of 2 ds, (p, 2 ds) 3 times, cl r; rw. Ch 6 ds, join in last p of prev lg ch. Rep from * until you are ready to work the last p of the 6th lg ch, fold-over join to first p of first lg ch. Ch 6 ds, rw. R of 2 ds, p, 2 ds, join in middle p of prev r, 2 ds, p, 2 ds, cl r; rw. Ch 4 ds, join to p of corresp ch. Ch 8 ds, join in next p on Center Ring. Cut and tie.

Glue the stones to the chains in the center of the snowflake.

Lacy Snowflake

Approximately 3½" point to point

Materials:
Size 10 white thread.
2 shuttles.

Wind 1 yd. on Sh #1, do not cut; wind 8½ yds. on Sh #2. Picot spacing is ½".

Center Ring: *Sh #1*, r of 2 ds, (p, 2 ds) 5 times, cl r. Tie shuttle threads together to form 6th p. Count knot as first half of next ds.

Sections: *Sh #1*, ch 9 ds. *Sh #2*, r of 4 ds, (p, 4 ds) 3 times, cl r. *R of 4 ds, join to last p of prev r, (1 ds, p) 10 times, 4 ds, cl r.** R of 4 ds, join to last p of prev r, (4 ds, p) twice, 4 ds, cl r. *Sh #1*, ch 9 ds, join to same p on Center Ring as before, ch 3 ds, join to next p on Center Ring. Ch 9 ds. *Sh #2*, r of 4 ds, p, 4 ds, join to middle p of prev r, 4 ds, p, 4 ds, cl r. Rep from * 4 more times. For 5th rep, work up to **, make r of 4 ds, join to last p of prev r, 4 ds, fold-over join to middle p of first r, 4 ds, p, 4 ds, cl r. *Sh #1*, ch 9 ds, join to same p on Center Ring as before. Ch 3 ds, join to first ds. Cut and tie.

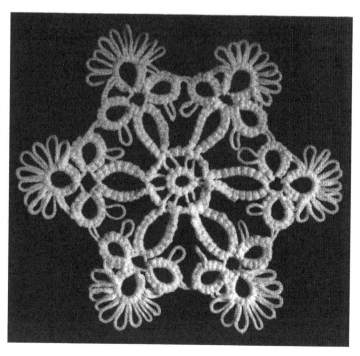

Three-Dimensional Snowflake #1

Three-Dimensional Snowflake #2

Three-Dimensional Snowflake #1

Approximately 4″ in diameter

Materials:
Size 20 white thread.
Shuttle.

12″ of ⅟₁₆″-wide red satin ribbon.
Glue (hot glue gun recommended).

Rnd 1: Wind 1½ yds. on shuttle, do not cut; use ball thread.
*R of 2 ds, (p, 2 ds) 3 times, cl r; rw. Ch 3 ds, rw. Rep from * 5 more times, join ch to base of first r. Cut and tie.
Rnd 2: Wind 7 yds on shuttle, do not cut; use ball thread. Lg p spacing is ½″.
R of 3 ds, (p, 3 ds) 3 times, cl r; rw. Ch 6 ds, join to first p of any r on Rnd 1. Ch 1 ds, join to next p on next r on Rnd 1, 6 ds; rw. *R of 3 ds, p, 3 ds, join to middle p of prev r, 3 ds, p, 3 ds, cl r; rw. Ch 4 ds, p, 4 ds; rw. R of 1 ds, (lg p, 1 ds) 7 times, cl r; rw. Ch 4 ds, sm p, 2 ds; rw. R of 1 ds, (lg p, 1 ds) 9 times, cl r; rw. Ch 2 ds, join to sm p of prev ch, 4 ds; rw. R of 1 ds, (p, 1 ds) 7 times, cl r; rw. Ch 4 ds, join to p of corresp ch on opposite side, 4 ds; rw.** R of 3 ds, (p, 3 ds) 3 times, cl r; rw. Ch 6 ds, sk 1 p on same r on Rnd 1, join to next p. Ch 1 ds, join to next p on next r on Rnd 1. Ch 6 ds, rw. Rep from * 4 more times. Rep from * to ** once, join ch at base of first r. Cut and tie. Make three.

Starch and block snowflakes flat. When two are almost dry, fold them in half, matching the points. Roll two pieces of plastic wrap to measure 1″ in diameter by 4″ long and place one between the sides of each snowflake so that they dry in a V-shape. Leave the third snowflake to dry flat. When the snowflakes are completely dry, place a folded snowflake on each side of the flat one. Glue the centers together. Tie a loop in the center of the ribbon for a hanger and tie the ends in a bow around the center top of the ornament.

Three-Dimensional Snowflake #2

Approximately 4″ in diameter

Materials:
Size 20 white thread.
Shuttle.
12″ of ⅟₁₆″-wide red satin ribbon.
Glue (a hot glue gun is recommended).

Wind 7 yds. on shuttle, do not cut, use ball thread.
R of 3 ds, p, 3 ds, sm p, 3 ds, p, 3 ds, cl r; rw. Lg ch of 6 ds, sm p, 6 ds, lg p, 6 ds, sm p, 6 ds; rw. *R of 3 ds, p, 3 ds, join to sm p of prev r, 3 ds, p, 3 ds, cl r; rw. Ch 5 ds, sm p, 5 ds; rw. R of 2 ds, (p, 2 ds) 5 times, cl r; rw. Ch 3 ds, p, 3 ds; rw. R of 2 ds, (p, 2 ds) 5 times, cl r; rw. Ch 3 ds, join to p of prev ch, 3 ds; rw. R of 2 ds, (p, 2 ds) 5 times, cl r; rw. Ch 5 ds, join to p of corresp ch on opposite side, 5 ds; rw.** R of 3 ds, p, 3 ds, sm p, 3 ds, p, 3 ds, cl r; rw. Lg ch of 6 ds, join to next sm p of prev lg ch, 6 ds, join in lg p of first ch, 6 ds, sm p, 6 ds; rw. Rep from * around up to 6th lg ch. To make 6th ch—6 ds, join to next p of prev lg ch, 6 ds, join in lg p of first ch, 6 ds, join in first p of first lg ch, 6 ds; rw. Then rep from * to **. Join at base of first r. Cut and tie. Make three.

Starch and block snowflakes flat. When two are almost dry, fold them in half, matching the points. Roll two pieces of plastic wrap to measure 1″ in diameter by 4″ long and place one between the sides of each snowflake so that they dry in a V-shape. Leave the third snowflake to dry flat. When the snowflakes are completely dry, place a folded snowflake on each side of the flat one. Glue the centers together. Tie a loop in the center of the ribbon for a hanger and tie the ends in a bow around the center top of the ornament.

Sparkling Snowflake

Approximately 1¼″ in diameter

Materials:
Size 30 white thread.
Shuttle.
Glue.
Glitter.

Wind 1½ yds. on shuttle, do not cut; use ball thread.
R of 2 ds, p, 3 ds, 3 lg p sep by 1 ds, 3 ds, p, 2 ds, cl r; rw. Ch 1 ds, tiny p, 1 ds; rw. (R of 2 ds, join to last p of prev r, 3 ds, 3 lg p sep by 1 ds, 3 ds, p, 2 ds, cl r; rw. Ch 1 ds, tiny p, 1 ds; rw) 4 times. R of 2 ds, join to last p of prev r, 3 ds, 3 lg p sep by 1 ds, 3 ds, fold-over join to first p of first r, 2 ds, cl r; rw. Ch 1 ds, tiny p, 1 ds; rw. Join at base of first r. Cut and tie.

Brush snowflake with glue and sprinkle with glitter.

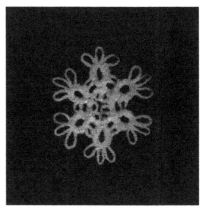

Sparkling Snowflake

Large Loop-Stitch Snowflake

Approximately 4½″ point to point

Materials:
Size 20 white thread.
2 shuttles.

Note: Spacing for the long picot (lg p) is 1″. To make the picots all the same size, cut a 1″-wide × 2″-long strip from a plastic lid. Place the plastic strip between the base thread and the thread coming from the shuttle. The strip should lie next to the last double stitch made. Holding the strip in place, make the next double stitch. Remove the plastic strip and push the stitches together to form the long picot.

Rnd 1: Wind 1½ yds. on shuttle, do not cut; use ball thread.
(R of 4 ds, lg p, 3 ds, lg p, 4 ds, cl r; rw. Ch 2 ds, p, 2 ds; rw) 6 times. Join at base of first r. Cut and tie—6 rings.

Rnd 2: Wind 3 yds. on shuttle, do not cut; use ball thread.

*R of 3 ds, lg p, 3 ds, p, 3 ds, lg p, 3 ds, cl r; rw. Ch 5 ds, *overlap 2 lg p of adjacent rings on Rnd 1 and join in both of them—loop st made*, ch 5 ds; rw. R of 3 ds, lg p, 3 ds, p, 3 ds, lg p, 3 ds, cl r; rw. Ch 4 ds, p, 4 ds; rw. Rep from * around, joining the ch-5 in the next 2 adjacent lg p on Rnd 1. Join at base of first r. Cut and tie.

Rnd 3: Wind 6 yds. on Sh #1, do not cut; wind 1 yd. on Sh #2.

Sh #1, r of 3 ds, (p, 3 ds) 3 times, cl r; *do not rw. Sh #2*, ch 3 ds, (p, 3 ds) 3 times; holding motif *below* chain, overlap 2 lg p of adjacent rings of Rnd 2 and join in both of them as follows: inserting point of shuttle through lps from front to back, draw up a lp and pass shuttle through lp from back to front. Ch 3 ds, (p, 3 ds) 5 times. Overlap next 2 adjacent lg p and join in both of them as before. Ch 3 ds, (p, 3 ds) 3 times. Rep from * around, join at base of first r. Cut and tie.

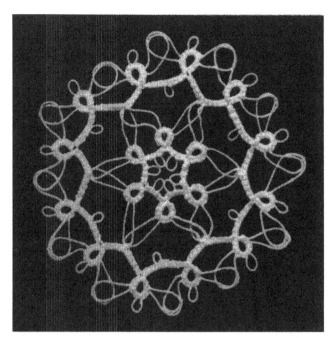

Small Loop-Stitch Snowflake

Small Loop-Stitch Snowflake

Approximately 3″ in diameter.

Materials:
Size 20 white thread.
Shuttle.

Work Rnds 1 and 2 of Large Loop-Stitch Snowflake. When blocking the snowflake, overlap the ends of the long picots on Rnd 2 so that they form circles.

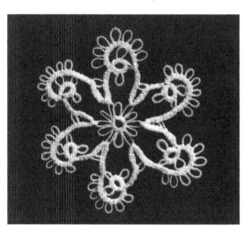

Whirlaway Snowflake

Whirlaway Snowflake

Approximately 2″ point to point

Materials:
Size 30 white thread.
Shuttle.

Wind 2 yds. on shuttle, do not cut; use ball thread.
Center Ring: R of 1 ds, (p, 1 ds) 11 times, cl r; tie ball and shuttle threads tog to form the 12th p; rw. Count knot as first half of next ds.

Rnd 1: Ch 5 ds, p, 4 ds; rw. *R of 3 ds, (p, 3 ds) 3 times, cl r; rw. Lg ch of 2 ds, (p, 2 ds) 7 times, join to middle p of prev r, ch 4 ds,** p, 5 ds, sk 1 p on Center Ring, join to next p. Ch 5 ds, join to p of prev ch, 4 ds; rw. Rep from * around, ending last rep at the **. Fold-over join to p of first ch, ch 5 ds, join to p at base of first ch. Cut and tie.

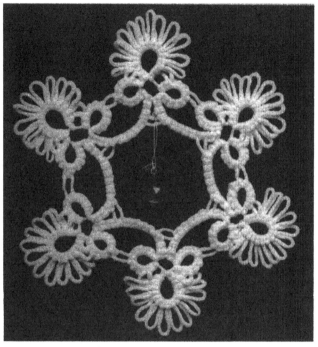

Crystal Petal Snowflake

Crystal Petal Snowflake

Approxmately 3¼″ point to point

Materials:
Size 10 white thread.
Shuttle.
One 10 mm crystal saucer bead.

Wind 7 yds. on shuttle, do not cut; use ball thread. Lg p has ½″ spacing.

R of 6 ds, p, 4 ds, p, 2 ds, cl r. *R of 2 ds, join to last p of prev r, (1 ds, lg p) 12 times, 1 ds, sm p, 2 ds, cl r. R of 2 ds, join to last p of prev r, 4 ds, p, 6 ds, cl r; rw.* Ch 3 ds, p, 6 ds, p, 3 ds; rw. R of 6 ds, join to last p of prev r, 4 ds, p, 2 ds; cl r. **Rep from * to * once more. Ch 3 ds, join to last p of prev ch, 6 ds, p, 3 ds; rw. R of 6 ds, join to last p of prev r, 4 ds, p, 2 ds, cl r.** Rep from ** to ** 3 more times. R of 2 ds, join to last p of prev r, (l ds, lg p) 12 times, 1 ds, sm p, 2 ds, cl r. R of 2 ds, join to last p of prev r, 4 ds, fold-over join to first p of first r, 6 ds, cl r; rw. Ch 3 ds, join to last p of prev ch, 6 ds, join to p of first ch, ch 3 ds, join at base of first r. Cut and tie.

Starch and block. When snowflake is dry, use fine sewing thread to hang the bead from a picot between chains.

Glittering Snowflake

Approximately 3" in diameter.

Materials:
Size 20 white thread.
Shuttle.
Glitter.
Glue.

Rnd 1: Wind 1 yd. on shuttle.
(R of 3 ds, p, 3 ds, cl r) 6 times. Cut and tie.
Rnd 2: Wind 1½ yds. on shuttle, do not cut; use ball thread.
R of 2 ds, p, 2 ds, join to p of any r on Rnd 1, 2 ds, p, 2 ds, cl r; rw. *Ch 3 ds, (p, 3 ds) 3 times; rw. R of 2 ds, p, 2 ds, join to p of next r on Rnd 1, 2 ds, p, 2 ds, cl r; rw. Rep from * 4 more times. Ch 3 ds, (p, 3 ds) 3 times; join at base of first r. Cut and tie.
Rnd 3: Wind 3 yds. on shuttle, do not cut; use ball thread.
R of 2 ds, (p, 2 ds) 3 times; rw. Ch 10 ds, join to first p worked of any ch on Rnd 2 *(see diagram)*. *Ch 3 ds, p, 3

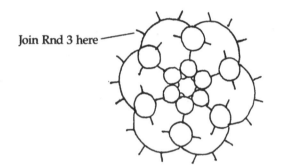

Join Rnd 3 here

ds; rw. R of 2 ds, (p, 2 ds) 3 times; rw. Ch 3 ds, p, 3 ds, join to first p of next ch on Rnd 2. Ch 10 ds, rw.** R of 2 ds, (p, 2 ds) 3 times; rw. Ch 10 ds, sk 1 p on Rnd 2, join in next p. Rep from * around, ending last rep at **, join at base of first r. Cut and tie.

Brush the snowflake with glue and sprinkle with glitter.

Miniature Snowflake

Approximately 2" point to point

Materials:
White tatting thread.
Shuttle.

Wind 3½ yds. on shuttle for Center Ring and Cloverleaves, do not cut; use ball thread.
Center Ring: R of 1 ds, (lg p, 1 ds) 11 times, cl r. Tie shuttle and ball threads together to form 12th p; rw. Count knot as first half of next ds. Ch 7 ds, rw.
Cloverleaf #1: R of 2 ds, (p, 2 ds) 5 times; cl r. *R of 2 ds, join to last p of prev r, (2 ds, p) 4 times; 2 ds, cl r.* Rep from * to * once more; rw. Ch 7 ds, sk 1 p on Center Ring, join to next p, 7 ds; rw.
Cloverleaf #2: R of 2 ds, p, 2 ds, join to next to last p of prev r, (2 ds, p) 3 times; 2 ds, cl r. Rep from * to * of first Cloverleaf twice; rw. Ch 7 ds, sk 1 p on Center Ring, join to next p, 7 ds; rw.
Cloverleaves #3, 4 and 5: Rep Cloverleaf #2.
Cloverleaf #6: Rep Cloverleaf #2 up to the next to last p of the last r, fold-over join to 2nd p of first r, 2 ds, p, 2 ds, cl r; rw. Ch 7 ds, join to p at base of first ch. Cut and tie.

Double Star Snowflake

Approximately 4″ point to point

Materials:
Size 10 white thread.
Shuttle.

Rnd 1: Wind 1½ yds. on shuttle.
R of 2 ds, (p, 2 ds) 3 times, cl r. *R of 2 ds, join to last p of prev r, (2 ds, p) twice, 2 ds, cl r. Rep from * for 5 rings. Make 6th r of 2 ds, join to last p of prev r, 2 ds, p, 2 ds, fold-over join to first p of first r, 2 ds, cl r. Join at base of first r. Cut and tie.

Rnd 2: Wind 2 yds. on shuttle, do not cut; use ball thread.
Join thread in p between any 2 rings. Ch 7 ds, rw. *R of 2 ds, (p, 2 ds) 3 times, cl r; rw. Ch 7 ds, join in next p between rings, 7 ds; rw. Rep from * around. Join in p where first joining was made. Cut and tie.

Rnd 3: Wind 3 yds. on shuttle, do not cut; use ball thread.

Join thread in last p of any r *(see diagram)*. *Ch 7 ds, rw. R of 2 ds, (p, 2 ds) 3 times, cl r; rw. Ch 7 ds, sk 1 p on r, join in next p, ch 2 ds, p, 2 ds; rw. R of 2 ds, (p, 2 ds) 3 times, cl r; rw. Ch 2 ds, p, 2 ds, join in first p of next r. Rep from * around. Cut and tie.

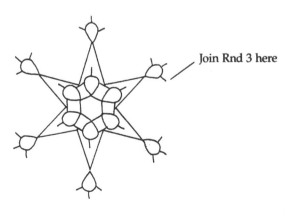

Join Rnd 3 here

Ribbon Snowflake

Approximately 2¾" in diameter

Materials:
White ribbon floss.
Shuttle.

Rnd 1: Wind 2 yds. on shuttle, do not cut; use ball thread.

R of 2 ds, (p, 4 ds) twice, p, 2 ds, cl r; rw. *Ch 2 ds, rw. R of 2 ds, join to last p of prev r, (4 ds, p) twice, 2 ds, cl r; rw. Rep from * 3 more times. Ch 2 ds, rw. For 6th r, make 2 ds, join to last p of prev r, 4 ds, p, 4 ds, fold-over join to first p of first r, 2 ds, cl r; rw. Ch 2 ds, join at base of first r. Cut and tie.

Rnd 2: Wind 2 yds. on shuttle, do not cut; use ball thread.

R of 3 ds, join to middle p of any r on Rnd 1, 3 ds, cl r; rw. *Ch 3 ds, p, 2 ds, medium p, 2 ds, lg p, 2 ds, medium p, 2 ds, p, 3 ds; rw. R of 3 ds, join to same p as before, 3 ds, cl r; rw. Ch 2 ds, (p, 2 ds) 3 times; rw.** R of 3 ds, join to middle p of next r on Rnd 1, 3 ds, cl r; rw. Rep from * around, ending last rep at **. Join ch at base of first r. Cut and tie.

Note: Do not starch snowflake as it takes away the sheen of the ribbon.

Ribbon Snowflake

Large Crystal Snowflake

Approximately 4¾" point to point

Materials:
Size 20 white thread.
Shuttle.
Crystal saucer bead.

Rnd 1: Wind 4 yds. on shuttle, do not cut; use ball thread.

R of 6 ds, p, 4 ds, p, 2 ds, cl r. *R of 2 ds, join to last p of prev r, (6 ds, p) twice, 2 ds, cl r. R of 2 ds, join to last p of prev r, 4 ds, p, 6 ds, cl r; rw.* Ch 3 ds, p, 6 ds, p, 3 ds; rw. R of 6 ds, join to last p of prev r, 4 ds, p, 2 ds, cl r. **Rep from * to * once. Ch 3 ds, join to last p of prev ch, 6 ds, p, 3 ds; rw. R of 6 ds, join to last p of prev r, 4 ds, p, 2 ds, cl r.** Rep from ** to ** 3 more times. R of 2 ds, join to last p of prev r, (6 ds, p) twice, 2 ds, cl r. R of 2 ds, join to last p of prev r, 4 ds, fold-over join to first p of first r, 6 ds, cl r; rw. Ch 3 ds, join to last p of prev ch, 6 ds, join to p of first ch, ch 3 ds, join at base of first r. Cut and tie.

Rnd 2: Wind 8 yds. on shuttle, do not cut; use ball thread.

R of 2 ds, p, (4 ds, p) twice, 2 ds, cl r; rw. Ch 2 ds, p, 2 ds; rw. R of 2 ds, join to last p of prev r, (6 ds, p) twice, 2 ds, cl r; rw. Ch 2 ds, p, 2 ds; rw. R of 2 ds, join to last p of prev r, (4 ds, p) twice, 2 ds, cl r; rw. Lg ch of 6 ds, p, 6 ds, join to any free p of middle r on Rnd 1, ch 3 ds, p, 3 ds; rw. **Rep * to * once. Ch 3 ds, p, 3 ds, join to free p of next middle r. Lg ch of 6 ds, p, 6 ds; rw. Rep from * to * once. Lg ch of 6 ds, join to p on prev lg ch, ch 6 ds, join to same middle p as before. Ch 3 ds, p, 3 ds; rw.** Rep from ** to ** 4 more times. Rep from * to * once. Ch 3 ds, p, 3 ds, join to same p as first joining. Ch 6 ds, join to p of first lg ch, 6 ds, join at base of first r. Cut and tie.

Starch and block. Fasten bead in center of snowflake with thread tied to a joining p on Rnd 1.

Swirl Snowflake

Approximately 4" in diameter

Materials:
Size 10 white thread.
2 Shuttles.

For Center Ring and Swirls, wind 4 yds. on Sh #1, do not cut; wind 4 yds. on Sh #2. Lg p has ½" spacing.

Center Ring: *Sh #1*, r of (1 ds, lg p) 11 times, 1 ds, cl r; tie shuttle threads tog to form 12th p; rw. Count knot as first half of ds.

Swirl No. 1: *Sh #1*, ch 3 ds, (p, 3 ds) 6 times; rw. *Sh #2*, start ch with a p (the last ch made will be joined to this p), *Sh #2*, ch 2 ds, p, 2 ds, join to last p of prev ch (*Note:* Sh #1 ch is below the work; insert shuttle from back to front through joining lp). (Ch 2 ds, p, 2 ds, join to next p on same ch) 5 times. Ch 2 ds, p, 2 ds, sk 1 p on Center Ring, join to next p; turn work over from right to left.

Start 2nd Swirl: *Sh #1*, ch (3 ds, p) 6 times, 3 ds; counting from Center Ring, sk 2 p of prev ch, join to next p; turn work over from right to left. Rep from * of Swirl #1 four more times. *Sh #2*, ch 2 ds, p, 2 ds, join to last p of prev ch, (ch 2 ds, p, 2 ds, join to next p on same ch) 3 times, 2 ds, fold-over join to end p on first ch, (*Note:* leaving the fold in place, work the remaining ch) ch 2 ds, join to next p of prev ch, 2 ds, p, 2 ds, join to next p on prev ch, 2 ds, p, 2 ds, join to p on Center Ring where first joining was made—6 swirls. Cut and tie.

Edging: Wind 1 yd. on shuttle, do not cut; use ball thread.

Join to first p of any swirl, *ch 2 ds, p, 2 ds, lg p, 2 ds, p, 2 ds, join to next p on same ch. Rep from * 2 more times, ch 3 ds, join to first p of next ch.** Rep from * to ** around, end by joining in first ds. Cut and tie.

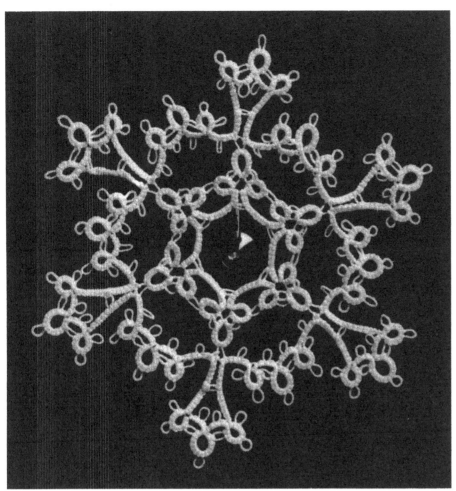

Large Crystal Snowflake

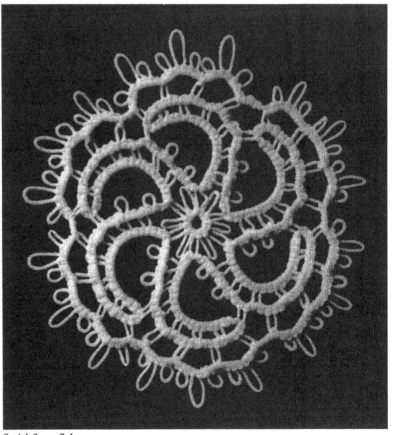

Swirl Snowflake

Daisy Snowflake

Approximately 3" in diameter

Materials:
Size 10 white thread.
Shuttle.

This snowflake is made with all chains.

Rnd 1: Wind 1 yd. on shuttle, do not cut; use ball thread. Make p at beg of ch. Ch 5 ds, p, 7 ds, (p, 2 ds) twice, p, 7 ds, p, 5 ds, join to p at beg of ch. *Ch 5 ds, join to last p of prev ch, 7 ds, (p, 2 ds) twice, p, 7 ds,** p, 5 ds, join to p at beg of first ch. Rep from * 3 more times. Rep from * to ** once, fold-over join to first p of first ch, ch 5 ds, join to beg p of first ch. Cut and tie.
Rnd 2: Wind 1 yd. on shuttle, do not cut; use ball thread. Lg p has ½" spacing.
Join thread to p between 2 chs. *Ch 6 ds, join to first p of next ch, ch 3 ds; (p, 1 ds) 9 times (making the first 5 picots graduated in size from small to large, the next 4 from large to small), 3 ds, sk 1 p on Rnd 1, join to next p, ch 6 ds, join to next p between chs. Rep from * 5 more times. Cut and tie.

Beaded Snowflake

Approximately 3¼" point to point

Materials:
Size 10 white thread.
Shuttle.
60 silver rocaille beads.

Rnd 1: String 6 beads on ball thread; moving beads along the thread, wind 3 yds. on shuttle, do not cut thread; use ball thread.
R of 5 ds, (p, 5 ds) 3 times, cl r; rw. Ch 1 ds, slide up a bead, 1 ds; rw. *R of 5 ds, join in last p of prev r, (5 ds, p) twice; 5 ds, cl r; rw. Ch 1 ds, slide up a bead, 1 ds; rw. Rep from * 3 more times. R of 5 ds, join to last p of prev r, 5 ds, p, 5 ds, fold-over join to first p of first r, 5 ds, cl r; rw. Ch 1 ds, slide up a bead, 1 ds, join to base of first r. Cut and tie.
Rnd 2: String 54 beads on ball thread; moving beads along the thread, wind 1 yd. on shuttle, do not cut thread; use ball thread.
Join thread in p between rings. *Ch 5 ds, (slide up a bead, 1 ds) 3 times; p, 3 ds, join in free p of next r on Rnd 1, 4 ds, join in p of prev ch, 6 ds, slide up 3 beads, 6 ds, p, 4 ds, join in same Rnd 1 p as before, 3 ds, join in p of prev ch, (1 ds, slide up a bead) 3 times, 5 ds, join in next p between rings. Rep from * around. Cut and tie.

Cloverleaf Snowflake

Cloverleaf Snowflake

Approximately 2″ point to point

Materials:
Size 30 white thread.
Shuttle.

Rnd 1: Wind 1 yd. on shuttle, do not cut; use ball thread.
R of 2 ds, (p, 2 ds) 3 times, cl r; rw. *Ch 2 ds, rw. R of 2 ds, join to last p of prev r, (2 ds, p) twice, 2 ds, cl r; rw. Rep from * 3 more times, ch 2 ds; rw. R of 2 ds, join to last p of prev r, 2 ds, p, 2 ds, fold-over join to first p of first r, 2 ds, cl r; rw. Ch 2 ds, join at base of first r. Cut and tie.
Rnd 2: Wind 3 yds. on shuttle, do not cut; use ball thread.
*R of 2 ds, (p, 2 ds) 3 times, cl r. R of 2 ds, join to last p of prev r, 2 ds, p, 2 ds, lg p, (2 ds, p) twice, 2 ds, cl r. R of 2 ds, join to last p of prev r, (2 ds, p) twice, 2 ds, cl r; rw. Ch 6 ds, join to middle p of any r on Rnd 1, 6 ds; rw. Rep from * 5 more times, joining ch to middle p of next r on Rnd 1. Join last ch at base of first r. Cut and tie.

Unique Snowflake

Approximately 2¼″ point to point

Materials:
Size 20 white thread.
Shuttle.

Wind 3 yds. of thread on shuttle.
R of 3 ds, (p, 3 ds) twice, cl r; rw. Leave ¼″ sp on shuttle thread. R of 3 ds, lg p, 3 ds, cl r; rw. *Leave ¼″ sp on shuttle thread. R of 3 ds, join to last p of next to last r, 3 ds, p, 3 ds, cl r. Leave ¼″ sp on shuttle thread. R of 3 ds, (p, 3 ds) 3 times, cl r. Leave ¼″ sp on shuttle thread. R of 3 ds, (p, 3 ds) twice, cl r; rw. Leave ¼″ sp on shuttle thread. R of 3 ds, join to lg p of 2nd r, 3 ds, cl r; rw. Rep

from * 4 more times. Leave ¼″ sp on shuttle thread. R of 3 ds, join to last p of next to last r, 3 ds, p, 3 ds, cl r. Leave ¼″ sp on shuttle thread. R of 3 ds, (p, 3 ds) 3 times, cl r. Leave ¼″ sp on shuttle thread, join at base of first r. Cut and tie.

Unique Snowflake

Feathery Snowflake

Approximately 2″ point to point

Materials:
Size 30 white thread.
2 shuttles.

Note: Picot spacing is ⅜″.
Center Ring: Wind 1 yd. on shuttle.
R of 1 ds, (lg p, 1 ds) 12 times, cl r. Cut and tie.
Rnd 1: Wind 1½ yds. on Sh #1, do not cut; wind 2½ yds. on Sh #2.
Sh #1, r of 5 ds, join to any p on Center Ring, 5 ds, cl r; rw. *Ch 2 ds, 3 p sep by 1 ds, 2 ds. *Sh #2*, r of 5 ds, p, 5 ds, cl r. *Sh #1*, ch 2 ds, 3 p sep by 1 ds, 2 ds; rw. R of 5 ds, sk 1 p on Center Ring, join in next p, 5 ds, cl r; rw. Rep from * 4 more times. Ch 2 ds, 3 p sep by 2 ds. *Sh #2*, r of 5 ds, p, 5 ds, cl r. *Sh #1*, ch 2 ds, 3 p sep by 1 ds, 2 ds, join at base of first ring. Cut and tie.

Feathery Snowflake

Light-and-Airy Snowflake

Textured Snowflake

Light-and-Airy Snowflake

Approximately 4½" point to point

Materials:
Size 10 white thread.
2 shuttles.

Rnd 1: Wind 1 yd. on shuttle. Lg p spacing is ¾".
R of 1 ds, (lg p, 1 ds) 12 times, cl r. Cut and tie.
Rnd 2: Wind 2½ yds. on shuttle.
*R of 3 ds, p, 3 ds, cl r; rw. Leave ½" sp on shuttle thread.
Sm r of 1 ds, join to any p on Rnd 1, 1 ds, cl r; rw. Leave ½" sp on shuttle thread. Rep from * around, joining sm r to next p on Rnd 1. Join at base of first r. Cut and tie.
Rnd 3: Wind 1½ yds. on Sh #1, do not cut; wind 4 yds. on Sh #2.
Sh #1, sm r of 1 ds, join to p of any r on Rnd 2, 1 ds, cl r; rw. *Ch 2 ds, 3 p sep by 3 ds, 2 ds; rw. R of 1 ds, join to p of next r on Rnd 2, 1 ds, cl r. Ch 3 ds, p, 3 ds, *Sh #2*, r of 2 ds, (p, 2 ds) 3 times, cl r. *Sh #1*, ch 3 ds, p, 3 ds;** rw. Sm r of 1 ds, join to p of next r on Rnd 2, 1 ds, cl r; rw. Rep from * around, end last rep at **, join at base of first sm r. Cut and tie.

Textured Snowflake

Approximately 4¾" point to point

Materials:
Size 10 white thread.
Shuttle.

Center Ring: Wind 1 yd. on shuttle, do not cut; use ball thread. Picot spacing is ½"
R of 2 ds, (p, 2 ds) 5 times, cl r. Tie shuttle and ball threads tog to form 6th p. Count knot as ½ ds in first group.
Note: 1 *group* = ch first half of ds 4 times, then last half of ds 4 times. A joining st does not count as ½ ds of a group.
Rnd 1: *Ch 2 groups, p, 2 groups, join in next p on Center Ring. Rep from * around—6 points. Cut and tie.
Rnd 2: Wind 6½ yds. on shuttle, do not cut; use ball thread. Lg p has ¾" spacing.
Join in p any ch on Rnd 1. Ch 2 ds, p, 2 ds; rw. *R of 3 ds, p, 3 ds, very sm p, 3 ds, p, 3 ds, cl r; rw. Ch 1 group; rw. R of 2 ds, join to last p of prev r, 2 ds, very sm p, 2 ds, p, 2 ds, cl r; rw. Ch 1 group, p, 1 group, lg p, 1 group, p, 1 group; rw. R of 2 ds, p, 2 ds, join to sm p of prev r, 2 ds, p, 2 ds, cl r; rw. Ch 1 group, rw. R of 3 ds, join to last p of prev r, 3 ds, join to sm p of next r, 3 ds, p, 3 ds, cl r; rw. Ch 2 ds, p, 2 ds, join to p of next ch on Rnd 1. Ch 2 ds, join to p of prev ch, 2 ds; rw. Rep from * around up to the last ch. Ch 2 ds, fold-over join to p of first ch, 2 ds, join to p at base of first ch. Cut and tie.

Victorian Snowflake

Approximately 3" point to point

Materials:
Ecru DMC Cebelia, size 20.
2 shuttles.
Three deep red ribbon roses with leaves.
Glue.

Rnd 1: Wind 1½ yds. on shuttle.
R of 3 ds, p, (4 ds, p) 5 times, 3 ds, cl r. R of 3 ds, join to last p of prev r, (4 ds, p) 5 times, 3 ds, cl r. R of 3 ds, join to last p of prev r, (4 ds, p) 4 times, 4 ds, fold-over join to first p of first r, 3 ds, cl r. Cut and tie.
Rnd 2: Wind 3 yds. on Sh #1, do not cut; wind 7 yds. on Sh #2.
Sh #1, r of 3 ds, p, 3 ds, join to last free p on any r on Rnd 1, 3 ds, p, 3 ds, cl r; rw. *Ch 2 ds, (p, 2 ds) twice; rw. R of 3 ds, join in last p of prev r, 3 ds, join in next p on Rnd 1, 3 ds, p, 3 ds, cl r; rw. Ch (2 ds, p) 3 times, 3 ds. *Sh #2*, r of 3 ds, join to last p of prev ch, (3 ds, p) twice, 3 ds, cl r. **R of 3 ds, join to last p of prev r, (3 ds, p) twice, 3 ds, cl r. Rep from ** once more. *Sh #1*, ch 3 ds, join to last p of prev r, (2 ds, p) twice, 2 ds; rw. R of 3 ds, join to last p of last Sh #1 r, 3 ds, join to next p on Rnd 1, 3 ds, p, 3 ds, cl r; rw. Rep from * 4 more times—5 points. For 5th repeat, ch 2 ds, (p, 2 ds) twice; rw. R of 3 ds, join to last p of prev r, 3 ds, join to next p on Rnd 1, 3 ds, join to first p of first r, 3 ds, cl r; rw. Ch (2 ds, p) 3 times, 3 ds. *Sh #2*, r of 3 ds, join to last p of prev ch, (3 ds, p) twice, 3 ds, cl r. **R of 3 ds, join to last p of prev r, (3 ds, p) twice, 3 ds, cl r. Rep from ** once more. *Sh #1*, ch 3 ds, join to last p of prev r, (2 ds, p) twice, 2 ds, join at base of first r. Cut and tie.

Starch and block. Glue ribbon rose and leaves to center of snowflake.

Victorian Snowflake

Jingle Bell Snowflake

Approximately 4" point to point

Materials:
Size 10 white thread.
Shuttle.
Jingle bell.

Rnd 1: Wind 2 yds. on shuttle, do not cut; use ball thread.
R of 6 ds, p, 6 ds, cl r; rw. *Ch 6 ds, p, 6 ds, join to p of r (r is below the ch); rw. R of 6 ds, p, 6 ds, cl r; rw. Rep from * 4 more times. Ch 6 ds, p, 6 ds, join to p of prev r and base of first r at the same time.

Rnd 2: Ch 3 ds, (p, 3 ds) 3 times, *join to p of next ch, ch 3 ds, (p, 3 ds) 3 times, join to p between rings, ch 3 ds, join to last p of prev ch, ch (3 ds, p) twice, 3 ds. Rep from * 4 more times, join to p of next ch, ch 3 ds, (p, 3 ds) twice; fold-over join to first p of first ch, ch 3 ds, join to p between chs in Rnd 1. Cut and tie.

Rnd 3: Wind 1 yd. on shuttle, do not cut; use ball thread.
Join thread in first free p of first ch (*see diagram*), *ch 3 ds, p, 3 ds, join to next p, ch 6 ds, p, 1 ds, lg p, 1 ds, p, 6 ds, join to next p. Ch 3 ds, p, 3 ds, join to next p on same ch. Ch 3 ds, join to first free p of next ch. Rep from * around. Cut and tie.

Fasten jingle bell so it hangs in the center of the snowflake.

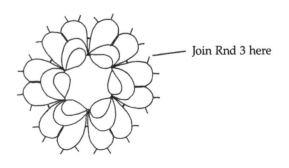

Join Rnd 3 here

Spoke Snowflake

Approximately 4″ point to point

Materials:
Size 10 white thread.
Shuttle.

Note: Lg p has ½″ spacing.

Rnd 1: Wind 2½ yds. on shuttle, do not cut; use ball thread.
R of 4 ds, (lg p, 2 ds) 3 times, lg p, 4 ds, cl r; rw. Ch 7 ds, p, 7 ds, rw. *R of 4 ds, (lg p, 2 ds) 3 times, lg p, 4 ds, cl r; rw. Ch 7 ds, join to p of first ch, 7 ds; rw. Rep from * 4 more times. Join ch at base of first r. Cut and tie.

Rnd 2: Wind 5 yds. on shuttle, do not cut; use ball thread.

R of 2 ds, (p, 2 ds) 3 times, cl r; rw. Ch 2 ds, join to 3rd p of any r on Rnd 1, ch 2 ds; rw. *R of 2 ds, join to last p of prev r, (2 ds, lg p) 3 times, 2 ds, p, 2 ds, cl r; rw. Ch 2 ds, join to next p of same r on Rnd 1, ch 2 ds; rw. R of 2 ds, join to last p of prev r, (2 ds, p) twice, 2 ds, cl r; rw. Ch 2 ds, join to last p of same r on Rnd 1, ch 3 ds, p, 3 ds, join to first p of next r on Rnd 1, ch 2 ds;** rw. R of 2 ds, (p, 2 ds) 3 times, cl r; rw. Ch 2 ds, join in next p of same r on Rnd 1, ch 2 ds; rw. Rep from * 5 more times, end last rep at **. Join at base of first r. Cut and tie.

Frosty Snowflake

Approximately 4″ point to point

Materials:
Size 10 white thread.
2 shuttles.
144 silver rocaille beads.

Note: b = slide a bead or beads up to last ds.

Rnd 1: String 6 beads on ball thread; moving beads along thread, wind 1½ yds. on shuttle, do not cut; use ball thread. Beads will be on ball thread.
*R of 2 ds, (p, 2 ds) 3 times, cl r; rw. Ch 2 ds, b, 2 ds; rw. Rep from * 5 more times, join at base of first r. Cut and tie.
Rnd 2: String 48 beads on ball thread. Moving beads along thread, wind 3 yds. on shuttle, do not cut; use ball thread.

*R of 3 ds, (p, 3 ds) 3 times; rw. Ch 2 ds, (b, 1 ds) 4 times, 1 ds, join to middle p of r on Rnd 1, 2 ds, (b, 1 ds) 4 times, 1 ds; rw. Rep from * 5 more times, joining ch to middle p of next r. End by joining to base of first r. Cut and tie.
Rnd 3: String 90 beads on ball thread. Moving beads along thread, wind 2 yds. on Sh #1, do not cut; wind 3 yds. on Sh #2, working the beads onto Sh #2.
Sh #1, join to first p of any r on Rnd 2, *ch 2 ds, (b, 1 ds) 6 times; 3 b, (1 ds, b) 6 times; 2 ds, sk 1 p on same r, join to next p; rw. *Sh #2*, ch 2 ds, (p, 2 ds) 5 times, join to first p of next r; rw. Rep from * around, join in same p as beg joining. Cut and tie.

Star-Shaped Snowflake

Approximately 4″ in diameter

Materials:
Size 20 white thread.
2 shuttles.

Rnd 1: Wind 2 yds. on shuttle, do not cut; use ball thread.

R of 5 ds, p, 5 ds, lg p, 5 ds, p, 5 ds, cl r; rw. *Ch 4 ds, (p, 4 ds) 3 times; rw. R of 5 ds, join to last p of prev r, 5 ds, join to lg p of first r, 5 ds, p, 5 ds, cl r; rw. Rep from * 2 more times. Ch 4 ds, (p, 4 ds) 3 times; rw. R of 5 ds, join to last p of prev r, 5 ds, join to lg p of first r, 5 ds, join to last p of first r, 5 ds, cl r; rw. Ch 4 ds, (p, 4 ds) 3 times. Join at base of first r; cut and tie.

Rnd 2: Wind 4 yds. on Sh #1, do not cut; wind 6 yds. on Sh #2.

Sh #1, r of 5 ds, join to middle p of any ch on Rnd 1, 5 ds, cl r; rw. *Ch 3 ds, (p, 3 ds) 3 times; rw. Lrg r of 5 ds, p, 5 ds, join to next p on same ch, 5 ds, p, 5 ds, cl r; rw. Ch 4 ds, p, 3 ds. *Sh #2*, r of 3 ds, join to p of prev ch, (3 ds, p) twice, 3 ds, cl r. R of 3 ds, join to last p of prev r, (5 ds, p) twice, 3 ds, cl r. R of 3 ds, join to last p of prev r, (3 ds, p) twice, 3 ds, cl r. *Sh #1*, ch 3 ds, join to last p of prev r, 4 ds, rw. Lrg r of 5 ds, join to last p of prev lrg r, 5 ds, join to first p of next ch, 5 ds, p, 5 ds, cl r; rw. Ch 3 ds, (p, 3 ds) 3 times; rw.** R of 5 ds, join in next p of same ch on Rnd 1, 5 ds, cl r; rw. Rep from * around, ending last rep at **. Join ch to base of first r; cut and tie.

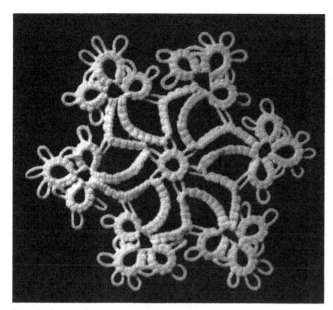

Pinwheel Snowflake

Pinwheel Snowflake

Approximately 3" point to point

Materials:
Size 10 white thread.
2 shuttles.

Center Ring: Wind 1 yd. on shuttle.
R of 1 ds, (p, 2 ds) 5 times, p, 1 ds, cl r. Cut and tie.
Rnd 1: Wind 6 yds. on Sh #1, do not cut; wind 2 yds. on Sh #2.
Make Cloverleaf as follows—*Sh #1*, r of 3 ds, (p, 3 ds) 3 times, cl r. R of 3 ds, join to last p of prev r, (2 ds, p) 4 times, 3 ds, cl r. R of 3 ds, join to last p of prev r, (3 ds, p) twice, 3 ds, cl r; rw—Cloverleaf made. Ch 10 ds (pull base thread lightly so that chain curves), join to any p on Center Ring; rw. *Sh #2*, ch 5 ds, join to last p of prev r. Ch 5 ds. *Make Cloverleaf as before. Ch 10 ds (pull base thread lightly so that chain curves), join to next p on Center Ring; rw. *Sh #2*, ch 5 ds, join to last p of prev r. Ch 5 ds. Rep from * 4 more times, join at base of first r. Cut and tie.

Simple Snowflake

Approximately 3" point to point

Materials:
Size 10 white thread.
Shuttle.

Center Ring: Wind 1 yd. on shuttle.
R of 1 ds, (p, 1 ds) 12 times; cl r tightly. Cut and tie.
Rnd 1: Wind 4 yds. on shuttle. Picot spacing is ½".
R of 2 ds, p, 2 ds, join in any p on Center Ring, 2 ds, p, 2

ds, cl r; rw. *Leave ½" space on base thread. R of 2 ds, (p, 2 ds) 5 times, cl r; rw. Leave ½" space on base thread. R of 2 ds, p, 2 ds, sk 1 p on Center Ring, join in next p, 2 ds, p, 2 ds, cl r; rw. Rep from * around until you have made 6 large rings, leave ½" on base thread, join at base of first r. Cut and tie.

Simple Snowflake

Dainty Snowflake

Approximately 1" in diameter.

Materials:
White tatting thread.
Shuttle.

Wind 1 yd. on shuttle, do not cut; use ball thread.
R of 2 ds, (p, 2 ds) 3 times, cl r; rw. Ch 2 ds, (p, 2 ds) 5 times; rw. *R of 2 ds, join to last p of prev r, 2 ds, (p, 2 ds) twice, cl r; rw. Ch 2 ds, (p, 2 ds) 5 times; rw. Rep from * 3 more times. R of 2 ds, join to last p of prev r, 2 ds, p, 2 ds, join to first p of first r, 2 ds, cl r; rw. Ch 2 ds, (p, 2 ds) 5 times, join at base of first r. Cut and tie.

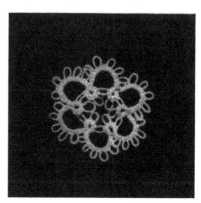

Dainty Snowflake